The Girl and the Block

Written by
Heidi Jenkins

Illustrated by
Renia Metallinou

Dedication:
For K.M.—the one who made
my dream come true and who
also inspired this story.

Challenge Words

were

tower

sister

rain

blue

A block sat all alone.

It sat in the backyard.

A boy named Tim put it there.

It sat for a long time.

Dad and a big dog saw it.

But no one took the block.

One day, it started to rain.

Tim's sister went to the backyard and saw the block.

She had seen
the block before.

It was muddy, and
it was not hers.

But the block had sat
for a long time now.

Tim did not play
with the block.

So now the girl took the old
block in with her.

She took off her wet hat and
her wet boots.

She took off her wet jacket
and wiped off the block.

Now it was clean and dry.

"Do you want this old block

from the yard?"

Tim did not want the block.

In her room the girl had more blocks.

She put the old
block with them.

The block did not look the
same as her blocks, but the
girl smiled.

In her mind she made the block a pretty brown color.

Now the block was a raft
she could ride on.

The raft took her down a
fast stream, and it was fun!

Now the block was red.

It was a pretty rose.

It had a great smell.

It made the girl smile.

She put the block on
more blocks.

Now it was part of
a tower.

The girl was a lady in the tower.

Big bears came to break
down the tower.

"Get them!" she told some of the blocks, which were her men.

She moved them to stop all the big, mad bears.

Then she made a big wall
out of blocks, and the bears
did not get in.

She was saved!

Next, the block
was a sled.

It took her for a ride
down the wall of blocks.

The girl had to hold on.

The ride was
long and bumpy,
but it was fun!

In the girl's mind, the soft snow hit her nose and made her smile.

She loved this block of hers.

The old block could be so
many things.

Soon all the blocks were blue, and the girl swam and smiled.

She saw cute fish.

She swam with a big ray.

Then the block was a truck, and the girl was in Africa.

From the truck, she saw lions and hippos.

Was that a zebra?

The girl turned the truck to see, but then she stopped.

"Time to eat!" the small girl's mom said from the hall.

Now the girl was
back in her room.

The blocks were just blocks.

The girl took the blocks and put them in a box.

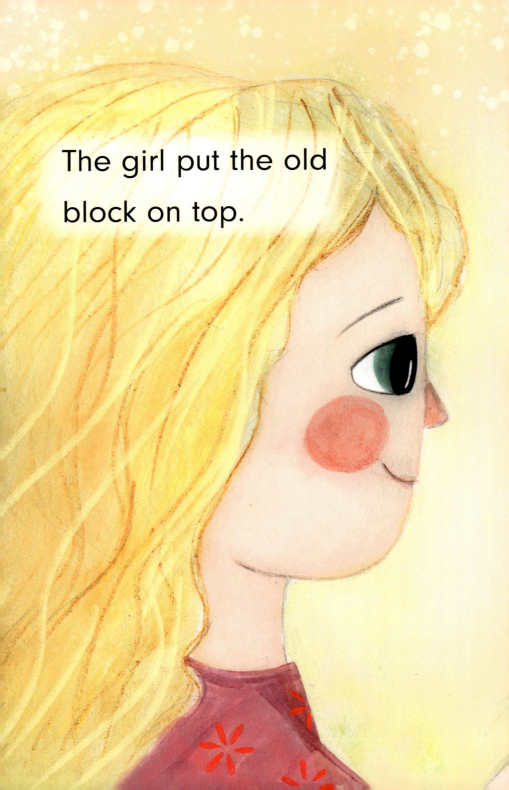

The girl put the old block on top.

She liked it best.

She had so much fun
with the block.

She did not care
that it was old.

The girl smiled.

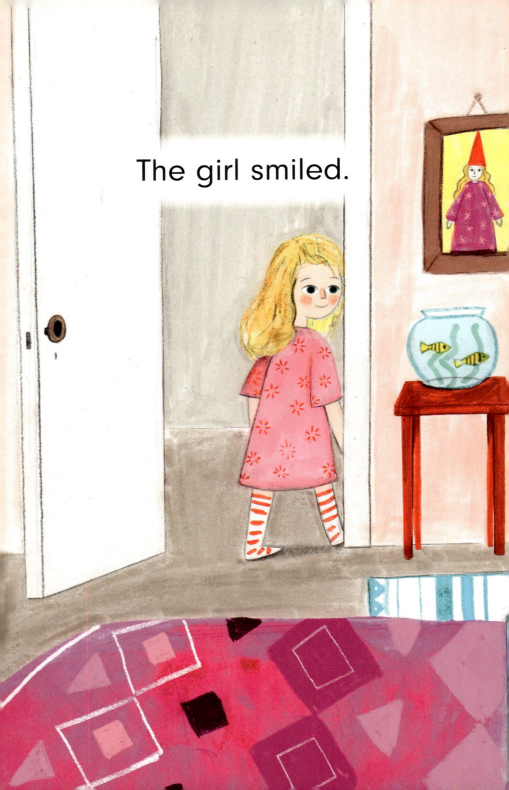

The old block was fun, just like all her pretty blocks.

More Books from
The Good and the Beautiful Library

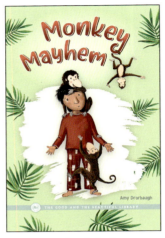

Monkey Mayhem
by Amy Drorbaugh

Brent's Bot
by Tessa Greene

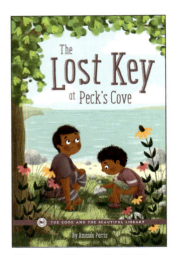

The Lost Key at Peck's Cove
by Amanda Parris

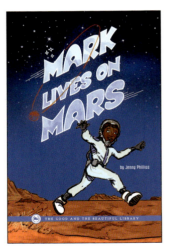

Mark Lives on Mars
by Jenny Phillips

goodandbeautiful.com